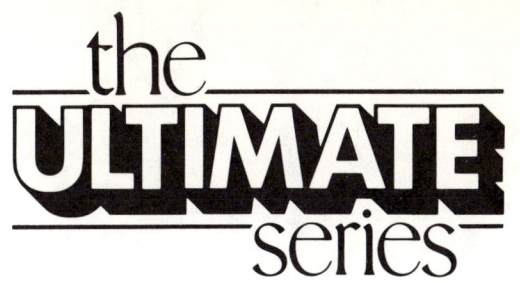

PIANO/VOCAL/GUITAR

JAZZ STANDARDS
100 GREAT JAZZ FAVORITES

HAL LEONARD PUBLISHING CORPORATION

Home Office:
960 East Mark Street
Winona MN 55987

National Sales Office:
8112 West Bluemound Road
Milwaukee WI 53213

For all works contained herein:
Unauthorized copying, arranging, adapting, recording or public performance is an infringement of copyright.
Infringers are liable under the law.

CONTENTS

- 10 Across The Alley From The Alamo
- 4 Ain't Misbehavin'
- 6 All Of Me
- 8 Among My Souvenirs
- 13 And All That Jazz
- 30 Angel Eyes
- 18 Au Privave
- 20 Bark For Barksdale
- 22 Bernie's Tune
- 24 Come Rain Or Come Shine
- 26 Cry Me A River
- 28 Cute
- 33 Day In The Life Of A Fool, A
- 42 'Deed I Do
- 36 Desafinado (Slightly Out Of Tune)
- 40 Dinner For One, Please James
- 45 Early Autumn
- 48 East Of The Sun (And West Of The Moon)
- 50 Five Brothers
- 52 Fly Me To The Moon
- 54 Foggy Day, A
- 57 From This Moment On
- 60 Girl From Ipanema, The
- 63 Gone With The Wind
- 66 Harlem Nocturne
- 69 Here's That Rainy Day
- 72 Honeysuckle Rose
- 74 How High The Moon
- 76 I Could Write A Book
- 78 I Got Plenty O' Nuttin'
- 83 I'll Remember April
- 90 I'll Take Romance
- 86 I'm Beginning To See The Light
- 88 I'm Sitting On Top Of The World
- 93 I've Got You Under My Skin
- 98 Imagination
- 101 "In" Crowd, The
- 102 Indiana (Back Home Again, Indiana)
- 104 Intermission Riff
- 106 It Ain't Necessarily So
- 112 It All Depends On You
- 114 It's A Blue World
- 134 It's All Right With Me
- 116 It's De-Lovely
- 118 It's Only A Paper Moon
- 120 Just In Time
- 122 Lady Is A Tramp, The
- 126 Let There Be Love
- 128 Let There Be You
- 130 Let's Get Away From It All
- 132 Li'l Darlin'
- 137 Love Is A Simple Thing
- 140 Love Is Blue
- 142 Lullaby Of The Leaves
- 146 Manhattan
- 149 Meditation
- 156 Moonglow
- 152 Moonlight In Vermont
- 154 More Than You Know
- 159 My Favorite Things
- 162 My Funny Valentine
- 164 Nice Work If You Can Get It
- 166 Night In Tunisia, A
- 182 Nightingale Sang In Berkeley Square, A
- 172 No Moon At All
- 174 Old Devil Moon
- 176 On A Clear Day
- 178 Ornithology
- 180 Our Day Will Come
- 185 Pennies From Heaven
- 188 Polka Dots And Moonbeams
- 191 Robbin's Nest
- 194 Route 66
- 197 Save The Bones For Henry Jones
- 200 Scrapple From The Apple
- 202 Silk Stockings
- 204 So Nice (Summer Samba)
- 207 Speak Low
- 210 Summertime
- 214 Sunday Kind Of Love, A
- 212 Sweet And Lovely
- 217 Sweetest Sounds, The
- 220 Taste Of Honey, A
- 222 That's All
- 225 There's A Small Hotel
- 228 They All Laughed
- 234 They Can't Take That Away From Me
- 230 Things We Did Last Summer
- 232 This Can't Be Love
- 237 Waltz For Debby
- 242 What A Diff'rence A Day Made
- 240 When I Fall In Love
- 245 Where Or When
- 248 Will You Still Be Mine
- 251 Willow Weep For Me
- 254 Wrap Your Troubles In Dreams
- 256 Yardbird Suite
- 258 You Turned The Tables On Me
- 262 You'd Be So Nice To Come Home To
- 260 You're The Cream In My Coffee

AIN'T MISBEHAVIN'

Words by ANDY RAZAF
Music by THOMAS WALLER and HARRY BROOKS

ALL OF ME

By SEYMOUR SIMONS
and GERALD MARKS

AMONG MY SOUVENIRS

Words by EDGAR LESLIE
Music by HORATIO NICHOLLS

ACROSS THE ALLEY FROM THE ALAMO

Words and Music by JOE GREENE

Copyright © 1947 by Michael H. Goldsen, Inc.
© Renewed 1975 Michael H. Goldsen, Inc.
International Copyright Secured   Made in U.S.A.   All Rights Reserved

AND ALL THAT JAZZ

Words by FRED EBB
Music by JOHN KANDER

AU PRIVAVE

By CHARLIE PARKER

BARK FOR BARKSDALE

By GERRY MULLIGAN

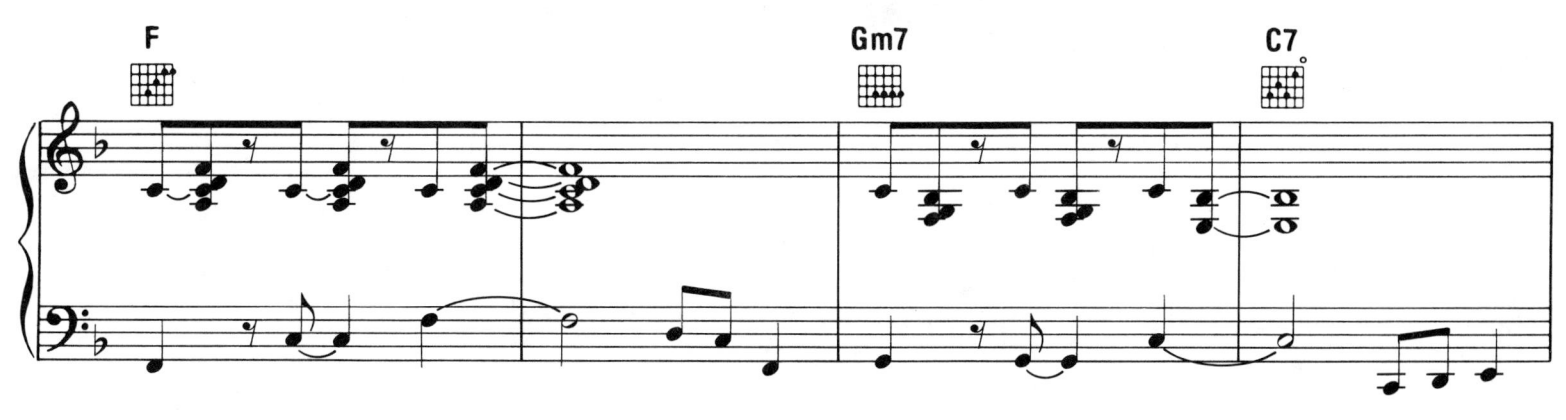
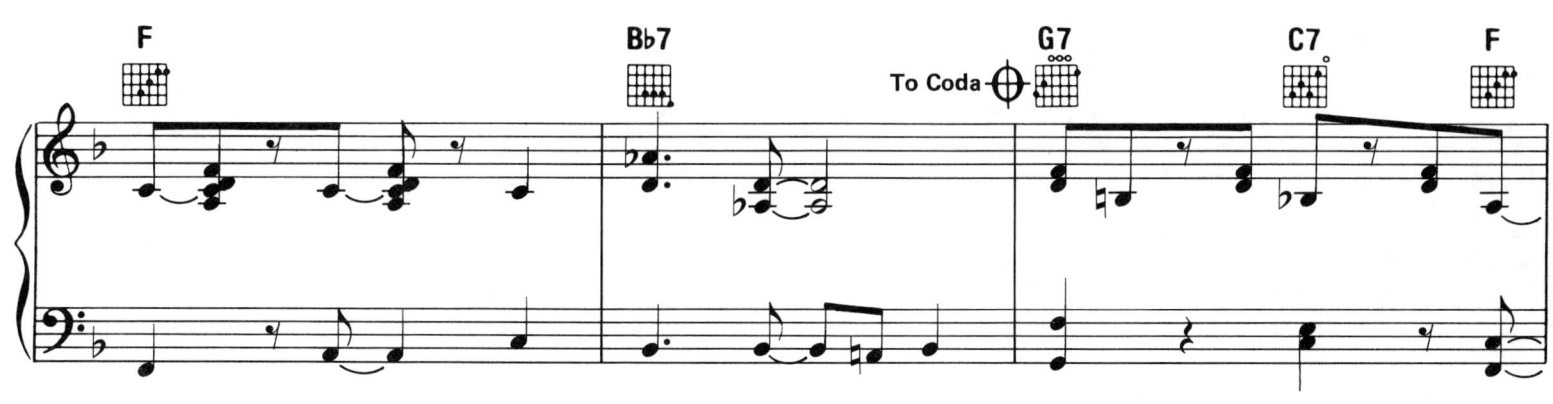
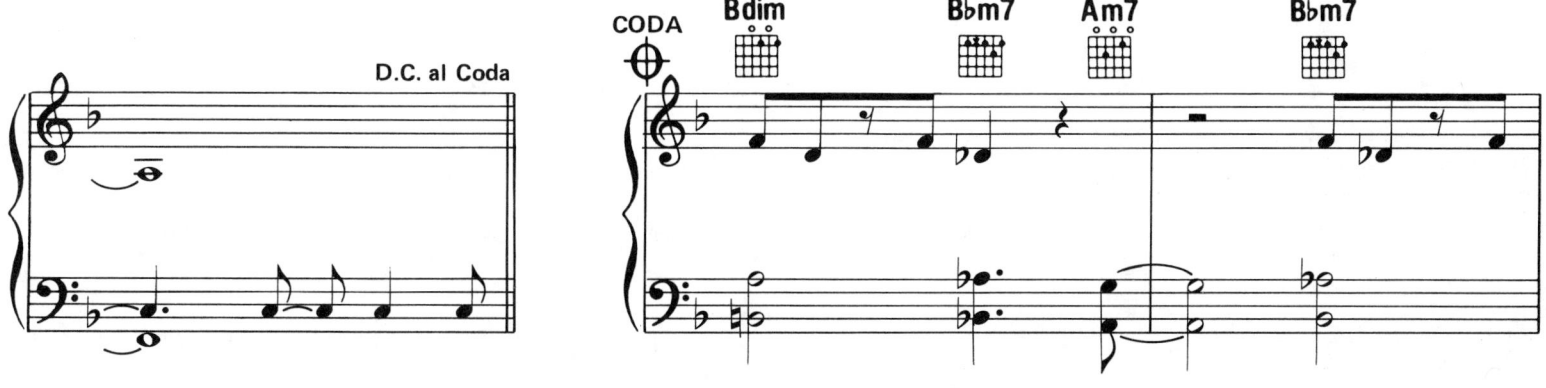
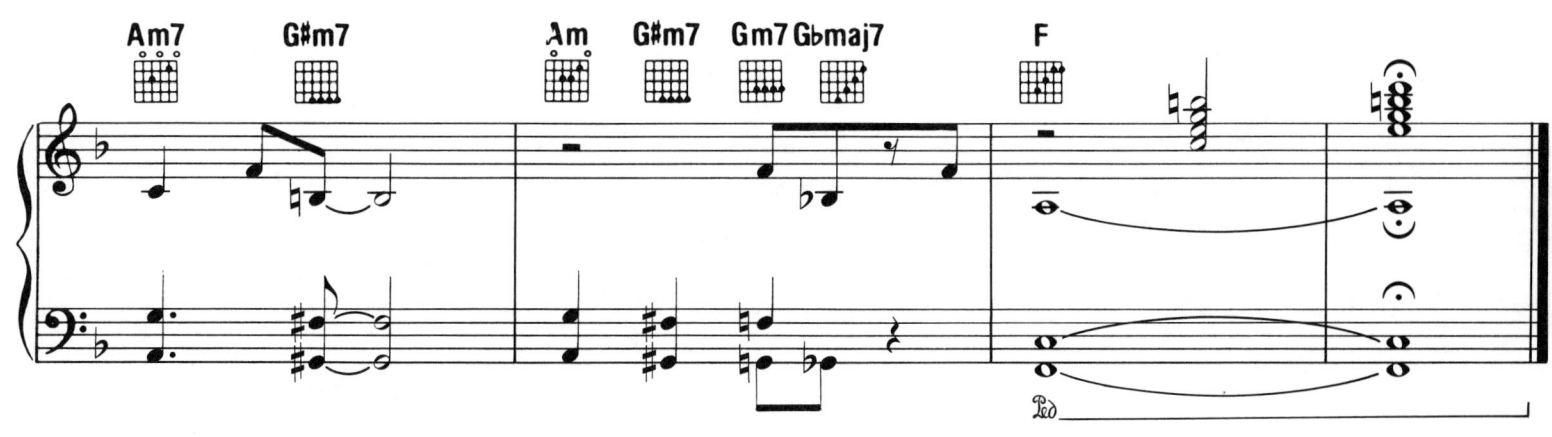

BERNIE'S TUNE

By BERNIE MILLER

Copyright 1953, 1954, 1955 by ATLANTIC MUSIC CORP.
International Copyright Secured   ALL RIGHTS RESERVED   Made in U.S.A.

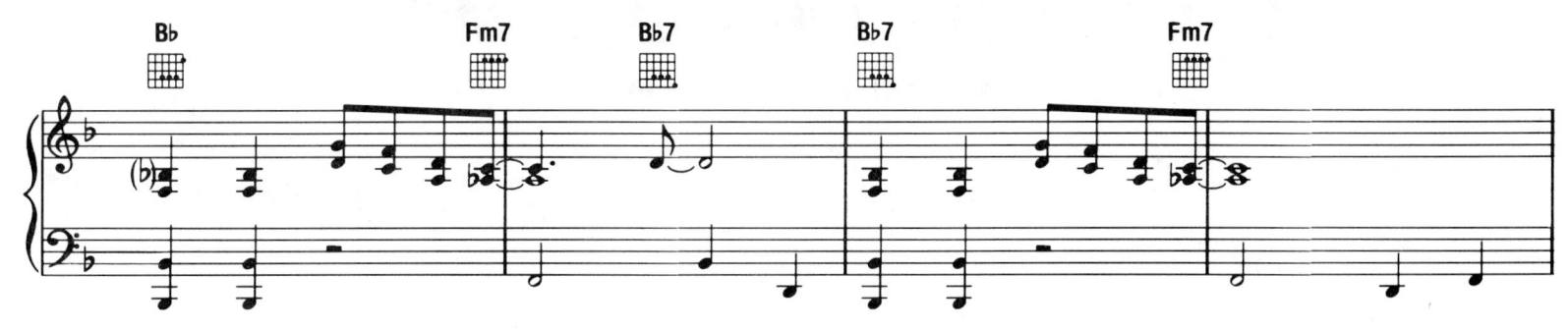
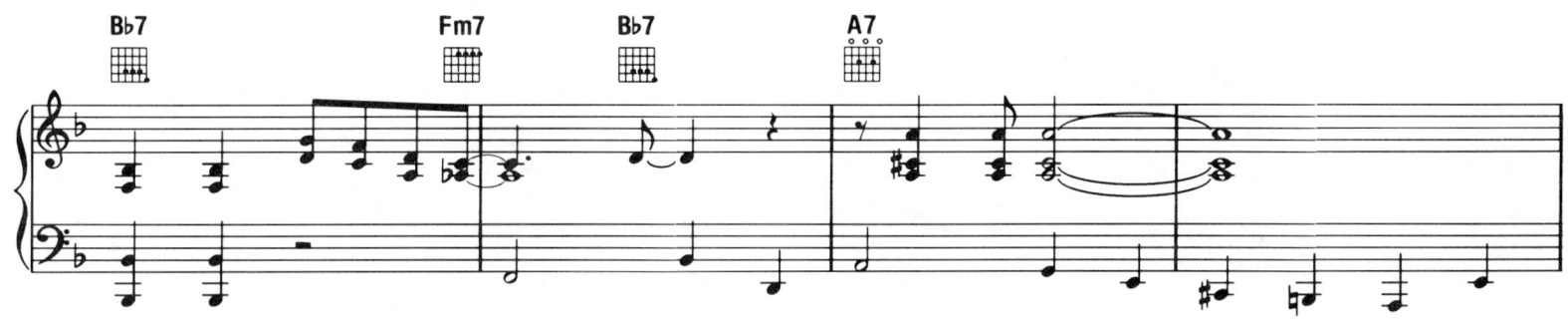
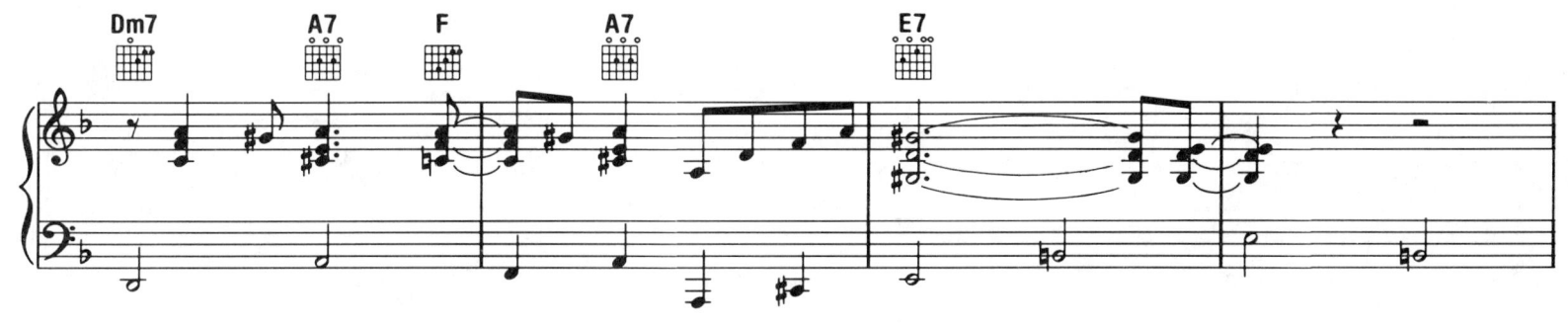
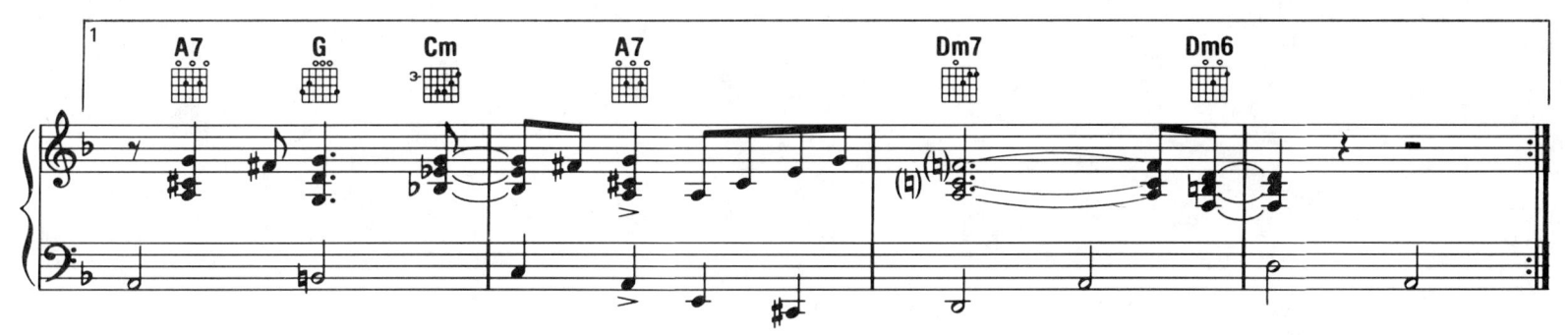
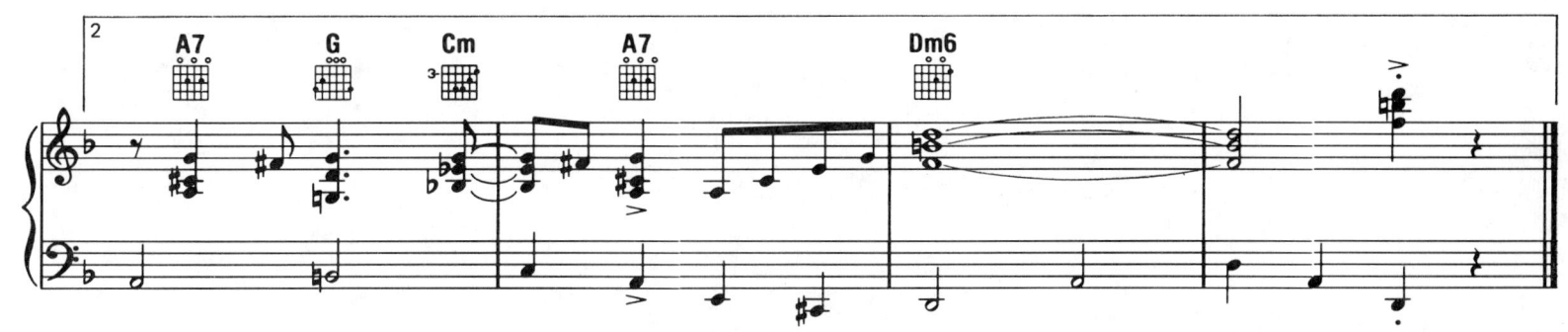

A Day in the Life of a Fool
(MANHÁ DE CARNAVAL)

Words by CARL SIGMAN
Music by LUIZ BONFA

Slow Bossa Nova

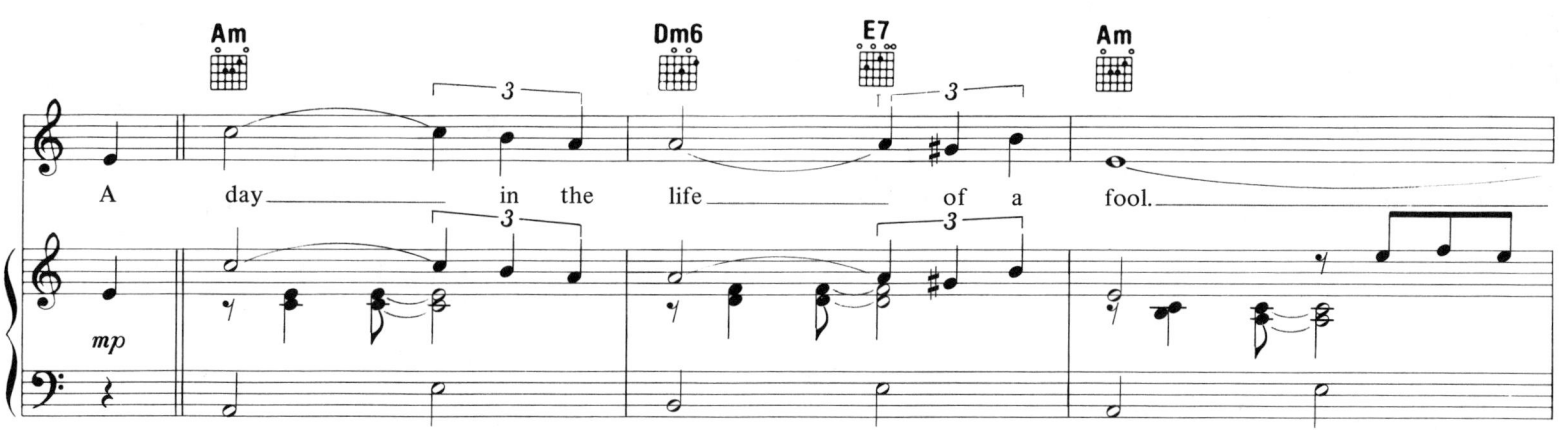

Copyright © 1959 by Nouvelles Editions Meridian
Copyright © 1964 by Anne-Rachel Music Corp. and United Artists Music Co., Inc.
Copyrights for the U.S.A. & Canada assigned to Chappell & Co., Inc. and United Artists Music Co., Inc.
All rights administered by Chappell & Co., Inc. (Intersong Music, Publisher)
International Copyright Secured   ALL RIGHTS RESERVED   Printed in the U.S.A.
Unauthorized copying, arranging, adapting, recording or public performance is an infringement of copyright.
Infringers are liable under the law.

DINNER FOR ONE, PLEASE JAMES

Words and Music by
MICHAEL CARR

'DEED I DO

EARLY AUTUMN

Words by JOHNNY MERCER
Music by RALPH BURNS
and WOODY HERMAN

Slowly, with feeling

When an Ear-ly Au-tumn walks the land ___ And chills the breeze And touch-es with her hand ___ the sum-mer trees, Per-haps you'll un-der-stand ___ What mem-o-ries I

TRO — © Copyright 1949 (Renewed 1977) and 1952 (renewed 1980) CROMWELL MUSIC, INC., New York, N.Y.
International Copyright Secured   Made in U.S.A.
All Rights Reserved Including Public Performance For Profit   Used by Permission

FIVE BROTHERS

Moderately

By GERRY MULLIGAN

GONE WITH THE WIND

By HERB MAGIDSON
and ALLIE WRUBEL

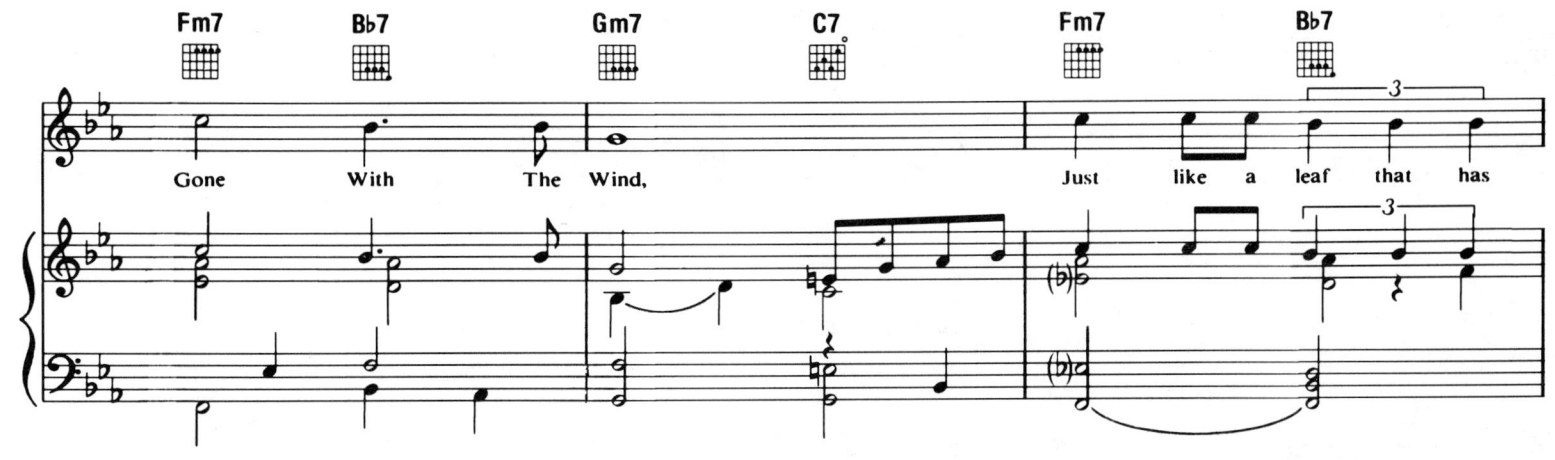

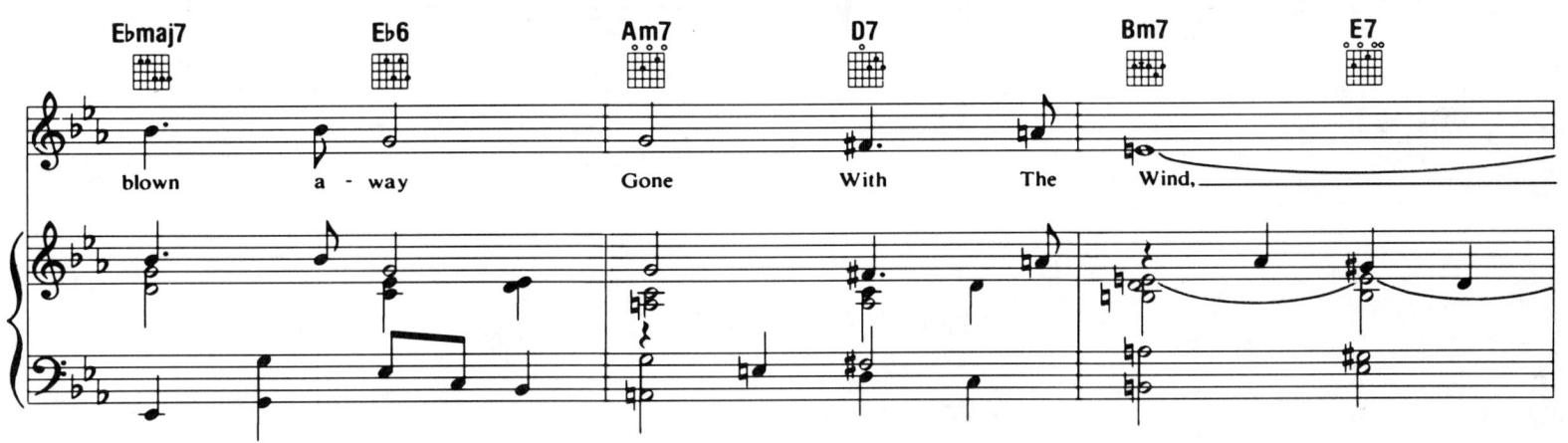

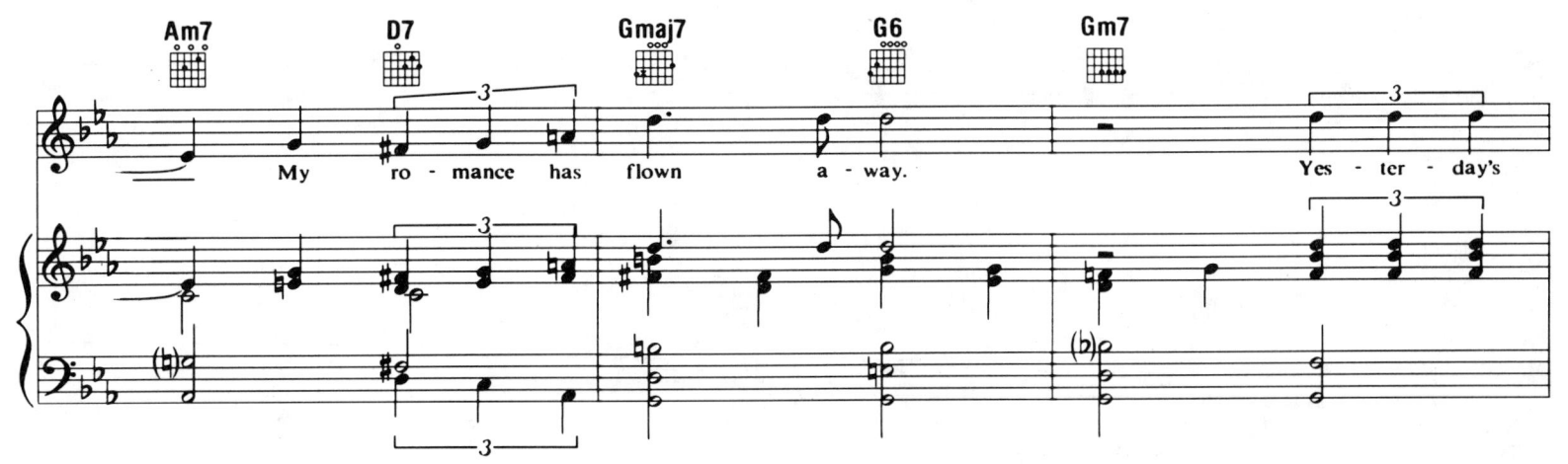

Copyright © 1937 by Bourne Co. Copyright Renewed.
This arrangement Copyright © 1982 by BOURNE CO.
All Rights Reserved.

HERE'S THAT RAINY DAY

Words by JOHNNY BURKE
Music by JAMES VAN HEUSEN

HONEYSUCKLE ROSE

Words by ANDY RAZAF
Music by THOMAS ("FATS") WALLER

HOW HIGH THE MOON
(From "TWO FOR THE SHOW")

Words by NANCY HAMILTON
Music by MORGAN LEWIS

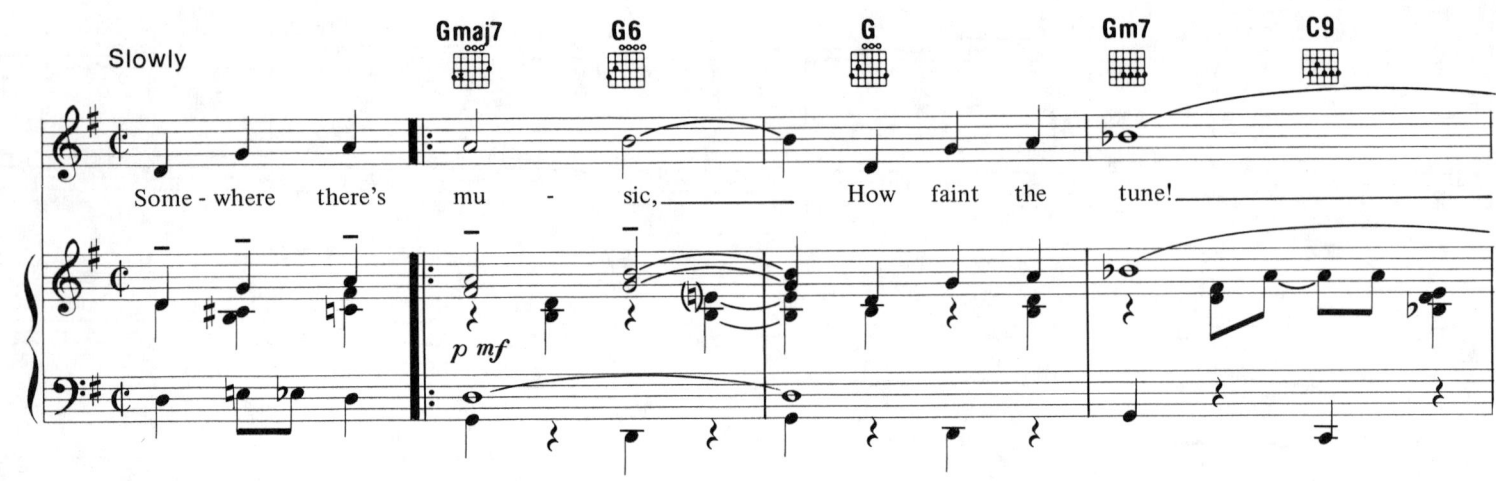
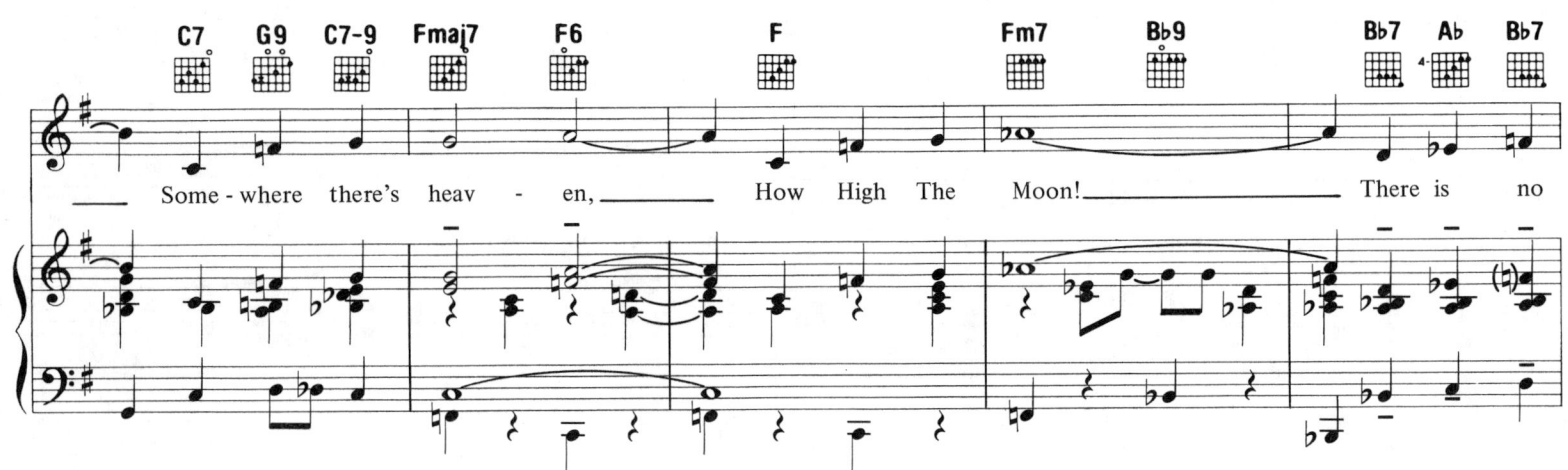

Copyright © 1940 by Chappell & Co., Inc.
Copyright Renewed
International Copyright Secured   ALL RIGHTS RESERVED   Printed in the U.S.A.
Unauthorized copying, arranging, adapting, recording or public performance is an infringement of copyright.
Infringers are liable under the law.

I COULD WRITE A BOOK
(From "PAL JOEY")

Words by LORENZ HART
Music by RICHARD RODGERS

I'LL REMEMBER APRIL

Words and Music by
DON RAYE, GENE DePAUL
and PAT JOHNSON

© Copyright 1941, 1942 by MCA MUSIC, A Division of MCA, Inc.
© Renewed 1969, 1970 PIC CORP.
Used by Permission   All Rights Reserved

I'M BEGINNING TO SEE THE LIGHT

Words and Music by HARRY JAMES,
DUKE ELLINGTON, JOHNNY HODGES
and DON GEORGE

I'LL TAKE ROMANCE

Words by Oscar Hammerstein II
Music by Ben Oakland

IMAGINATION

Words by JOHNNY BURKE
Music by JIMMY VAN HEUSEN

IT AIN'T NECESSARILY SO

Words by IRA GERSHWIN
Music by GEORGE GERSHWIN

Copyright © 1935 by Gershwin Publishing Corporation
Copyright Renewed, Assigned to Chappell & Co., Inc.
International Copyright Secured   ALL RIGHTS RESERVED   Printed in the U.S.A.
Unauthorized copying, arranging, adapting, recording or public performance is an infringement of copyright.
Infringers are liable under the law.

IT ALL DEPENDS ON YOU

Words and Music by
B.G. DeSYLVA, LEW BROWN
and RAY HENDERSON

IT'S A BLUE WORLD

Words and Music by
BOB WRIGHT and CHET FORREST

Copyright © 1939 by ABC Music Corp. and Bourne Co. Copyright Renewed.
This arrangement Copyright © 1982 by ABC Music Corp. and Bourne Co.
All Rights Reserved. International Copyright Secured.

IT'S ONLY A PAPER MOON

Words by BILLY ROSE and E.Y. HARBURG
Music by HAROLD ARLEN

JUST IN TIME
(From "BELLS ARE RINGING")

Words by BETTY COMDEN and ADOLPH GREEN
Music by JULE STYNE

Intro: Moderately

Just In Time, I found you Just In Time, Be - fore you came, my time was run - ning low. I was lost, The los - ing dice were tossed, My bridg - es all were crossed,

Copyright © 1956 by Betty Comden, Adolph Green and Jule Styne
Stratford Music Corporation, owner, and Chappell & Co., Inc. and G. Schirmer, Inc., Administrators of publication and allied rights.
International Copyright Secured   ALL RIGHTS RESERVED   Printed in the U.S.A.
Unauthorized copying, arranging, adapting, recording or public performance is an infringement of copyright.
Infringers are liable under the law.

LET THERE BE LOVE

Lyric by IAN GRANT
Music by LIONEL RAND

LI'L DARLIN'

By NEAL HEFTI

Moderately

IT'S ALL RIGHT WITH ME
(From "CAN-CAN")

Words and Music by
COLE PORTER

MANHATTAN

Words by LORENZ HART
Music by RICHARD RODGERS

We'll have Man - hat - tan   The Bronx and Stat - en   Is - land too;_____ It's love - ly
We'll go to Green - wich   Where mod - ern men itch   to be   free;_____ And Bowl - ing
We'll go to Yonk - ers   Where true love con - quers   in the   wilds;_____ And starve to -
We'll have Man - hat - tan   The Bronx and Stat - en   Is - land too;_____ We'll try to

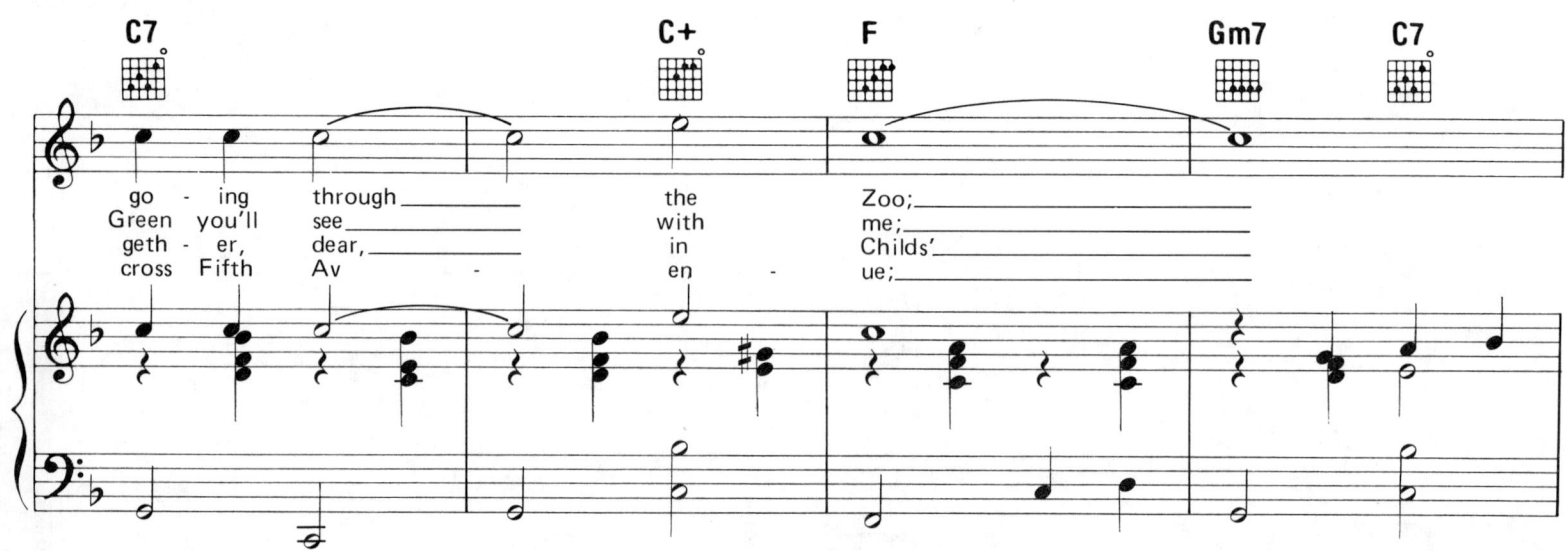

go - ing through_____ the   Zoo;_____
Green you'll see_____ with   me;_____
geth - er, dear,_____ in Childs'_____
cross Fifth Av - en - ue;_____

Copyright © 1925 by Edward B. Marks Music Corporation. Copyright renewed.
International Copyright Secured   Made in U.S.A.   All Rights Reserved
Used by permission

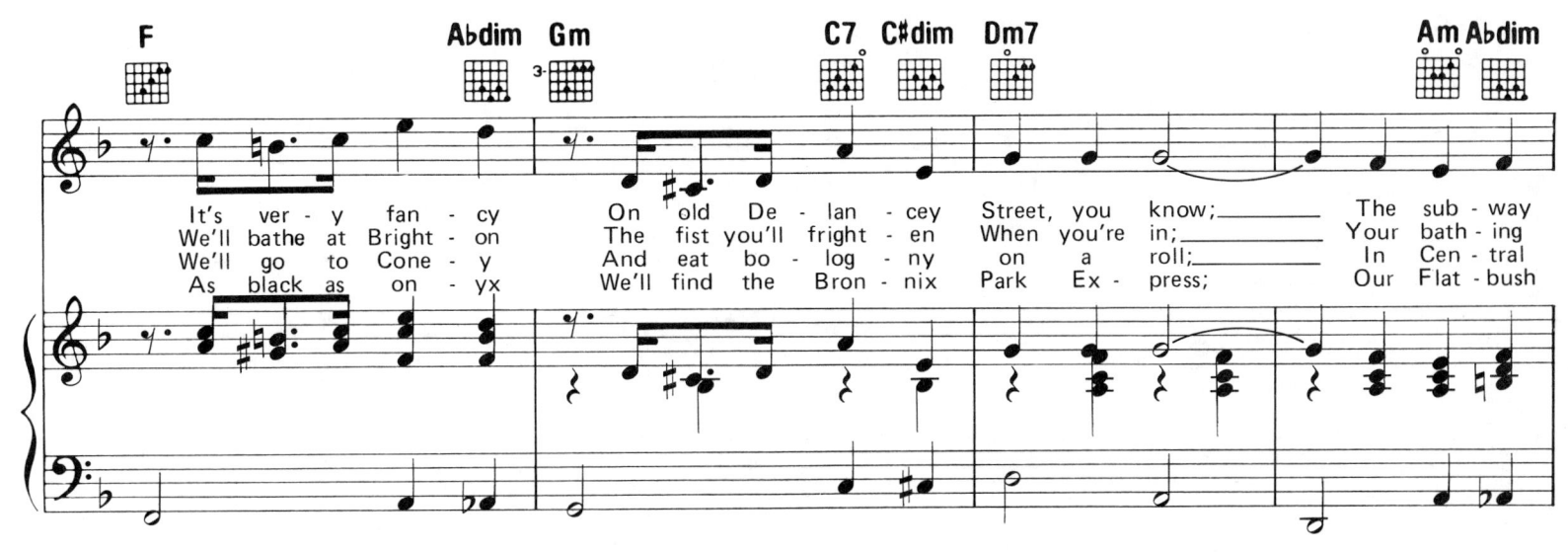
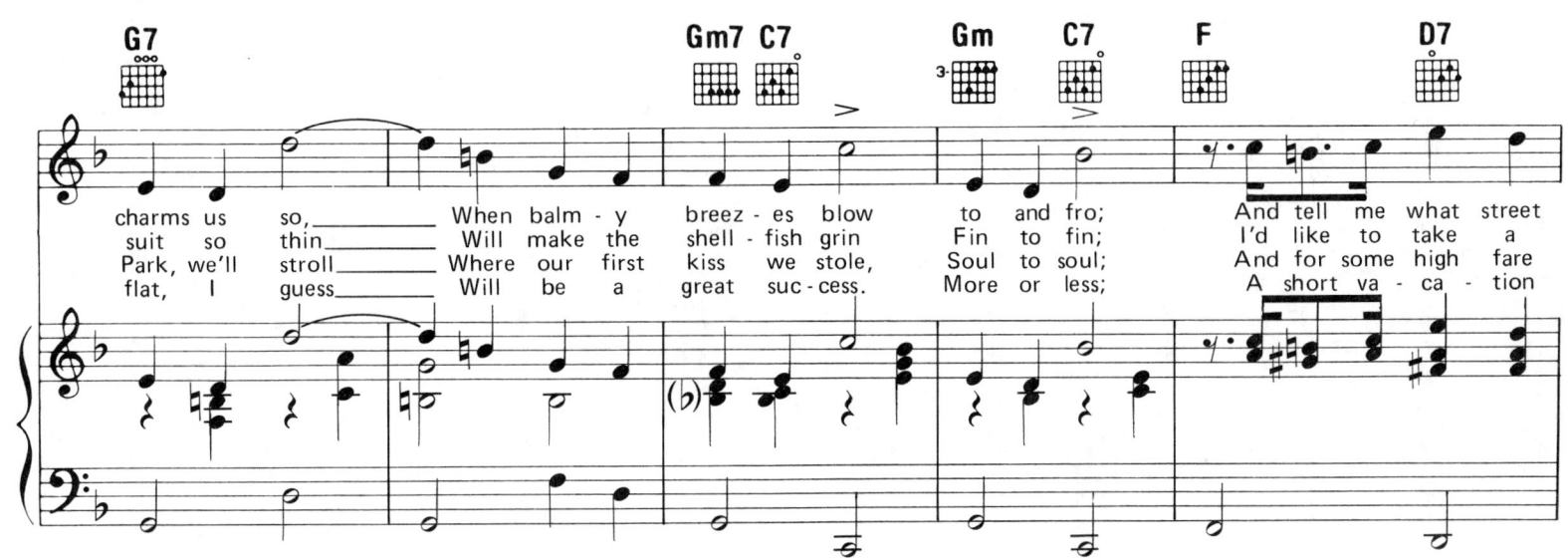
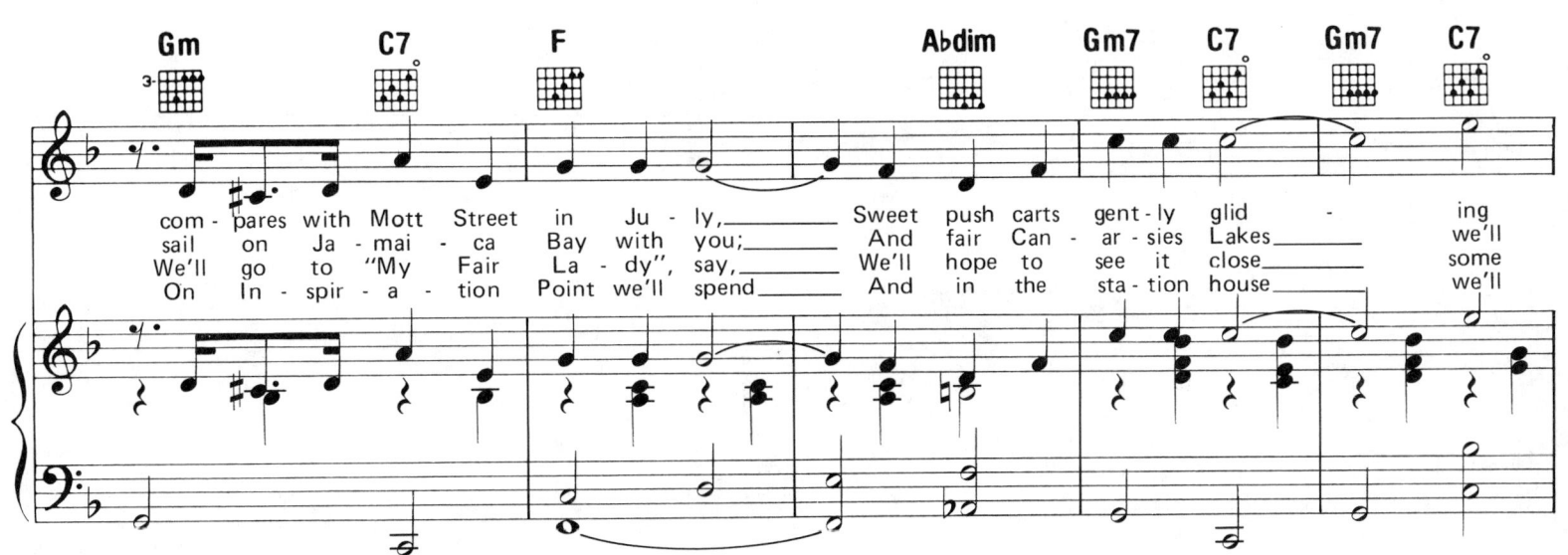

MOONGLOW

By WILL HUDSON, EDDIE DELANGE & IRVING MILLS

Copyright © 1934 by Mills Music, Inc. Copyright renewed.
Used with permission. All Rights Reserved.

NICE WORK IF YOU CAN GET IT

Words by IRA GERSHWIN
Music by GEORGE GERSHWIN

A NIGHT IN TUNISIA

by "DIZZY" GILLESPIE
and FRANK PAPARELLI

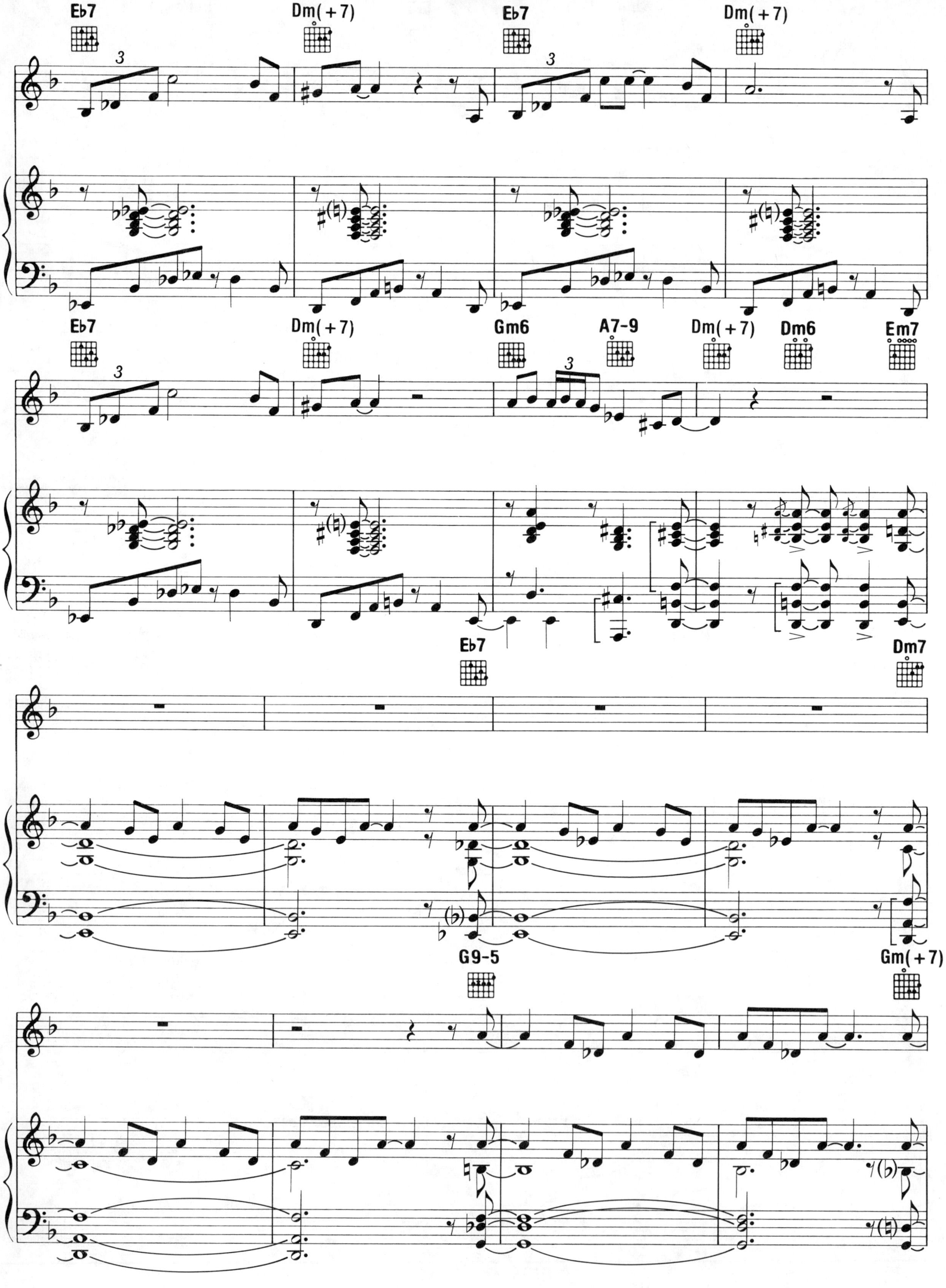
Eb7
Dm(+7)
Eb7
Dm(+7)
Eb7
Dm(+7)
Gm6
A7-9
Dm(+7)
Dm6
Em7
Eb7
Dm7
G9-5
Gm(+7)

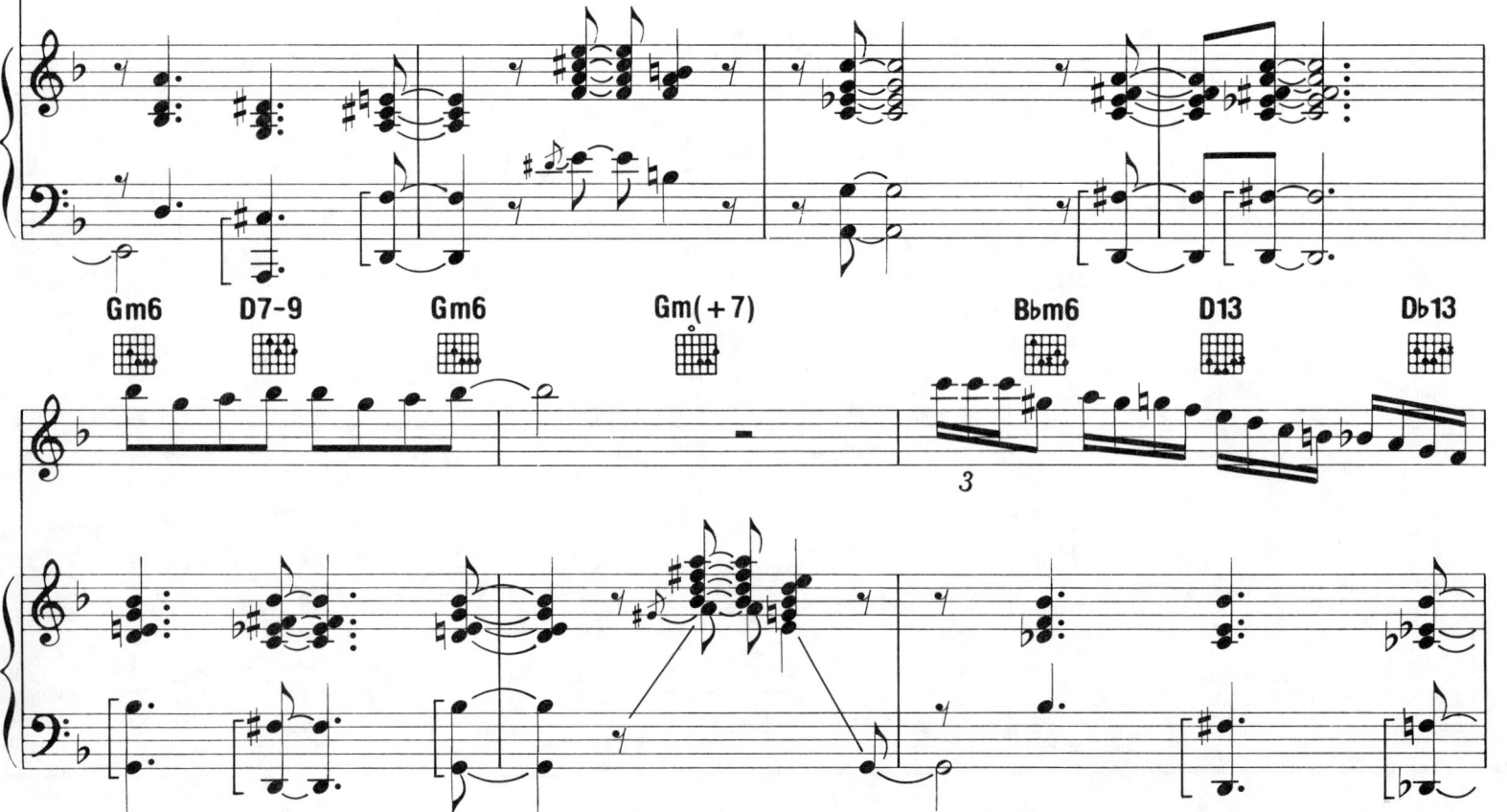

NO MOON AT ALL

Words and Music by
REDD EVANS and DAVE MANN

OLD DEVIL MOON
(From "FINIAN'S RAINBOW")

Words by E. Y. HARBURG
Music by BURTON LANE

POLKA DOTS AND MOONBEAMS

Words by JOHNNY BURKE
Music by JIMMY VAN HEUSEN

ROBBIN'S NEST

By SIR CHARLES THOMPSON
and "ILLINOIS" JACQUET

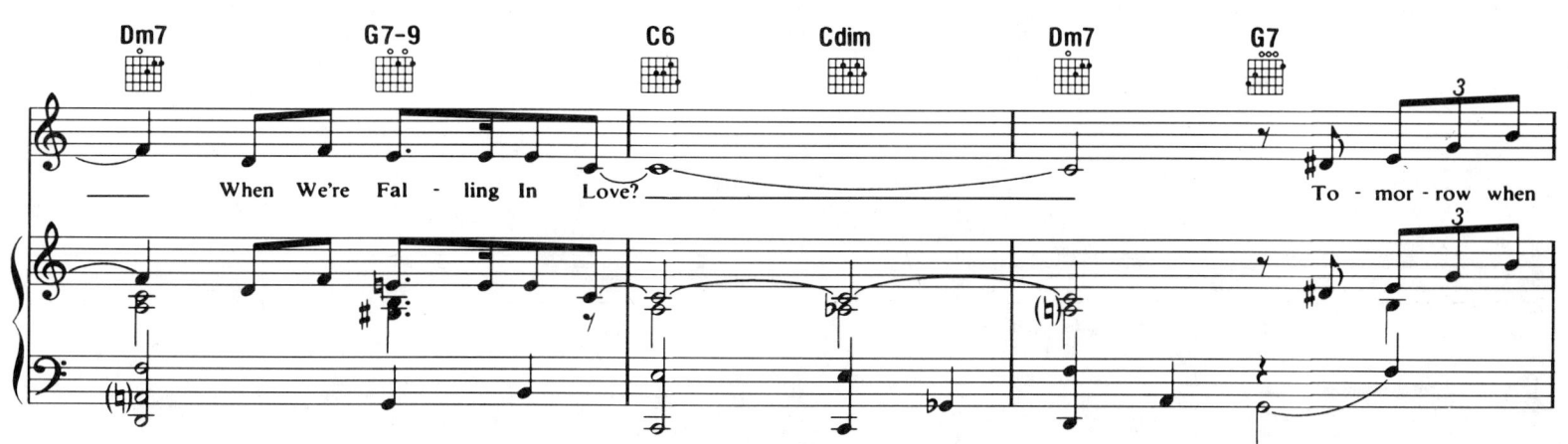

© 1947, 1948, 1951 and 1952 by Atlantic Music Corp.
© renewed and assigned 1975 by Atlantic Music Corp.
International Copyright Secured   Made in U.S.A.   All Rights Reserved

ROUTE 66

By BOBBY TROUP

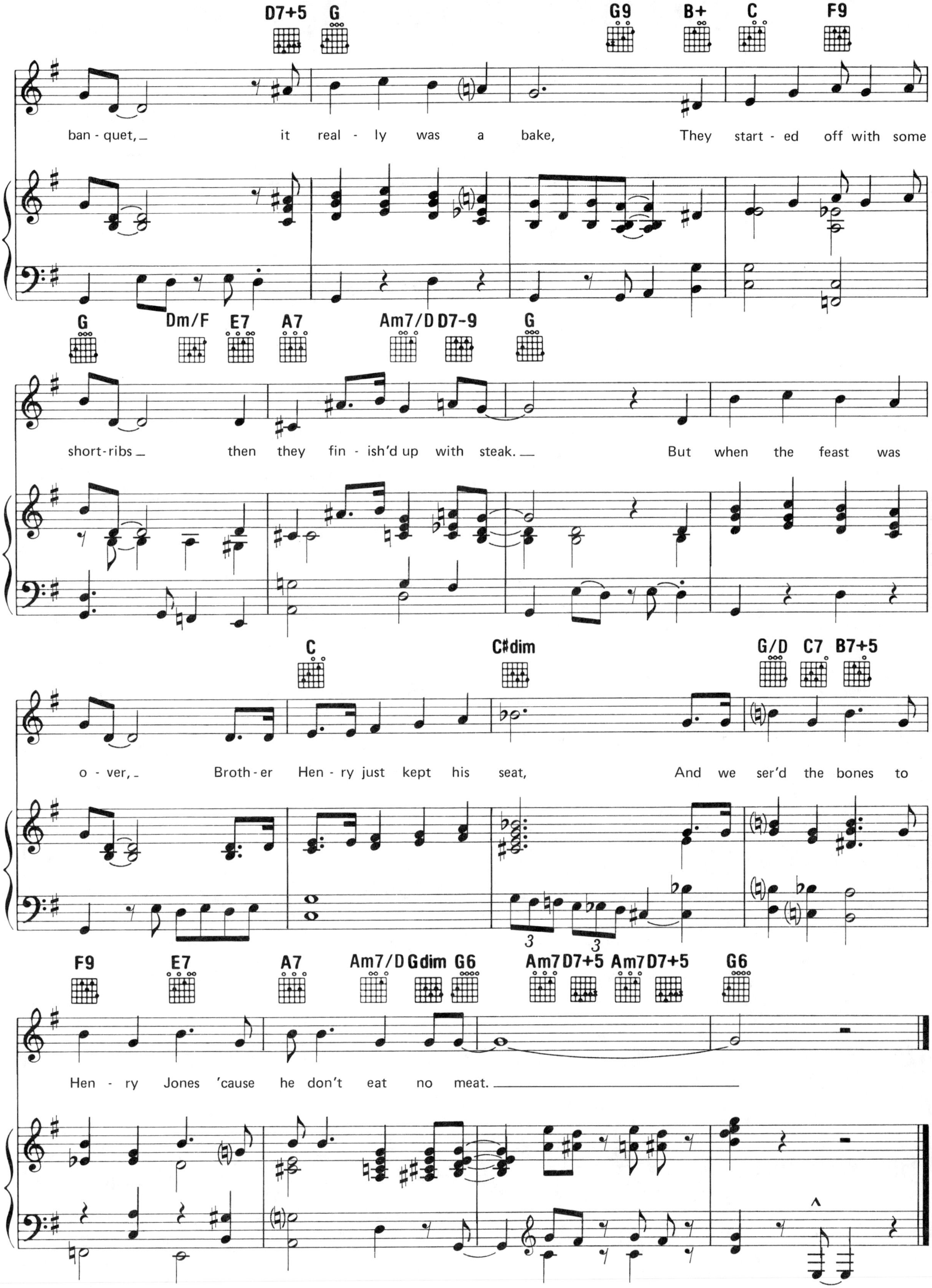
D7+5 G G9 B+ C F9
ban - quet, it real - ly was a bake, They start - ed off with some
G Dm/F E7 A7 Am7/D D7-9 G
short-ribs then they fin - ish'd up with steak. But when the feast was
C C♯dim G/D C7 B7+5
o - ver, Broth - er Hen - ry just kept his seat, And we ser'd the bones to
F9 E7 A7 Am7/D Gdim G6 Am7 D7+5 Am7 D7+5 G6
Hen - ry Jones 'cause he don't eat no meat.

SPEAK LOW
(From "ONE TOUCH OF VENUS")

Words by OGDEN NASH
Music by KURT WEILL

THEY ALL LAUGHED

Words by IRA GERSHWIN
Music by GEORGE GERSHWIN

WALTZ FOR DEBBY

Lyric by GENE LEES
Music by BILL EVANS

WHAT A DIFF'RENCE A DAY MADE

Lyric by STANLEY ADAMS
Music by MARIA GREVER

WILL YOU STILL BE MINE

Words by TOM ADAIR
Music by MATT DENNIS

WILLOW WEEP FOR ME

Words and Music by
ANN RONELL

YARDBIRD SUITE

By CHARLIE PARKER

YOU'D BE SO NICE TO COME HOME TO
(From "SOMETHING TO SHOUT ABOUT")

Words and Music by COLE PORTER

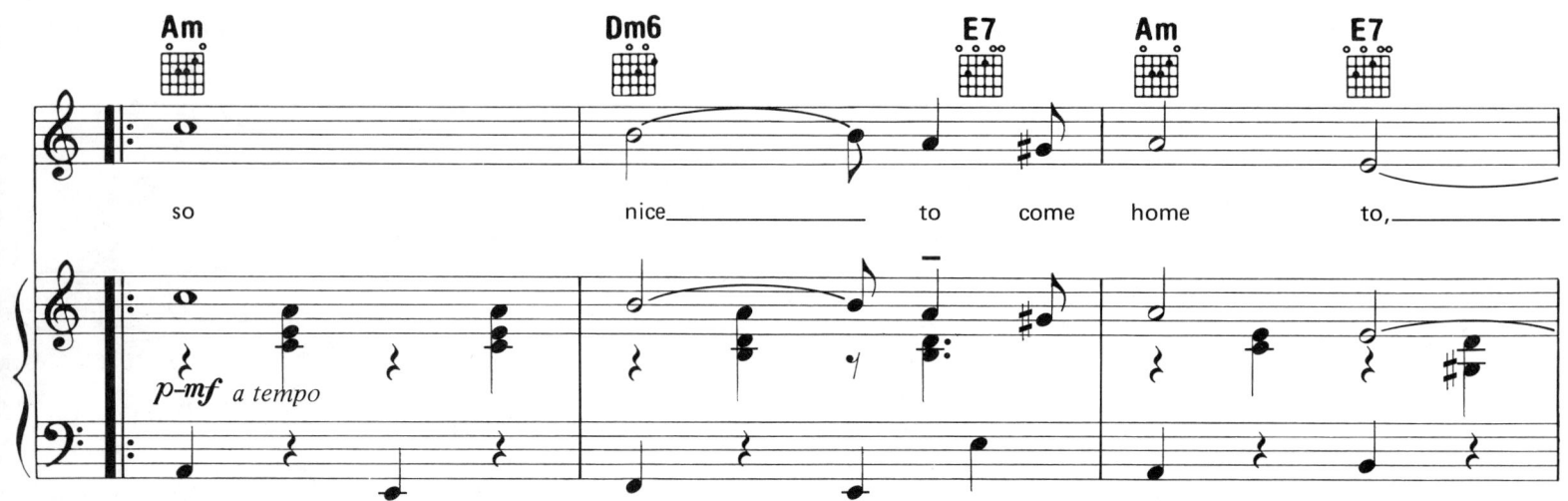

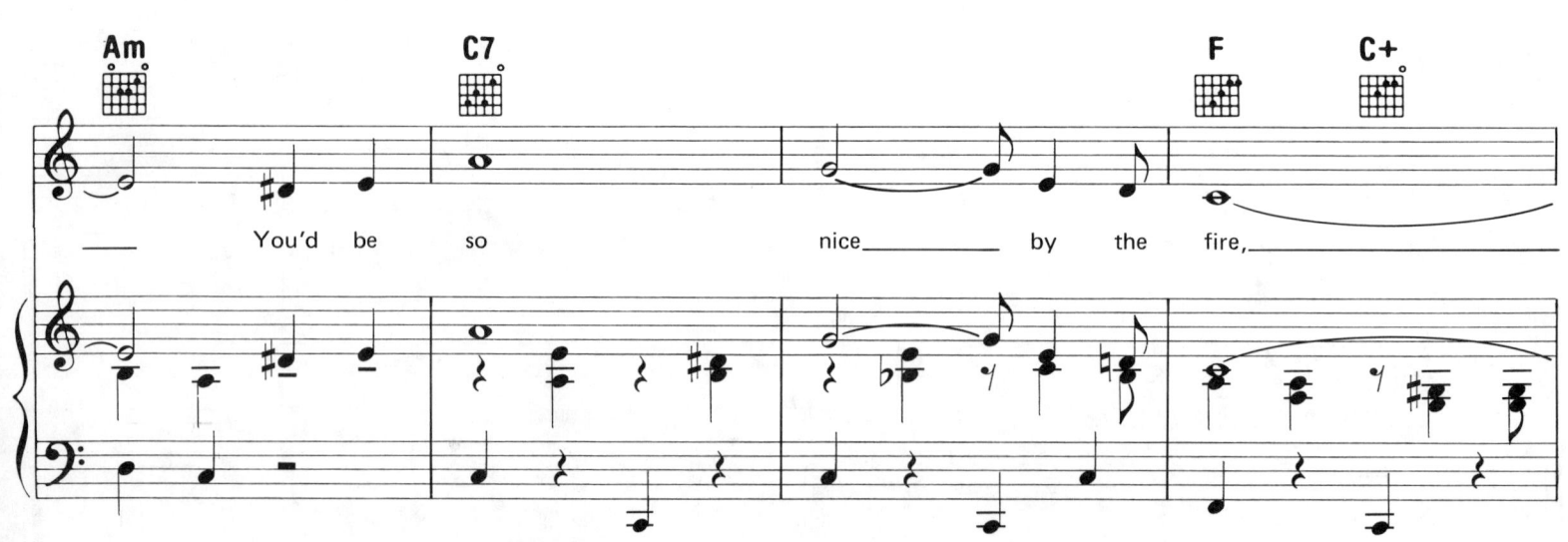

Copyright © 1942 by Chappell & Co., Inc. Copyright Renewed.
International Copyright Secured   ALL RIGHTS RESERVED   Printed in the U.S.A.
Unauthorized copying, arranging, adapting, recording or public performance is an infringement of copyright.
Infringers are liable under the law.